Peter Majoy

A BrainJoy Publication
Copyright 2018
Peter W. Majoy

*All Images are from
The Public Domain*

Design: Edward Morneau

ISBN-13: 978-1719482790

<u>Acknowledgements</u>

Pete Tandy,

for his inspirational contact

with the world including Coyotes;

Jean Tandy,

Pete's wonderful wife,

for her similar environmental connection

with life on Planet Earth;

and **Ed Morneau**

for his deep understanding

of the publishing process.

<u>Dedication</u>

To the world of nature and all those people,

like my loving family and friends,

who give so much to the animal kingdom

as a part of our environment

which we honor daily.

Peter Majoy

Contents

Coyote

<u>Introduction</u>

Some of the most wonderful people with whom I have made contact often had stories about their union with the natural world. Pete Tandy of Richmond, N.H. who passed away a number of years ago and who left a heart felt lasting impression within all who knew him was one of them. He wrote a piece in the November 1994 edition of the town publication, *The Richmond Rooster*, titled "The Coyote Pool" in which he describes a walk through the nearby woods in winter.

He described the many coyote tracks that led to and from a pool of water that never completely froze. It was then that he became aware of his cosmic connection with coyotes that resulted in his naming this body of water Coyote Pool.

At the end of his story, he wrote this: "... Here in the snow the story has unfolded. The coyotes have sat here long enough to melt the upper crystals of the snow. Just scratching fleas, you say? Oh, no. No tell-tale snow-fans from a flapping hind leg; nothing but stillness. Facing inward toward the pool. Watching something. Thinking of something. Dreaming of something...I see where they have sat before the pool, and know a kinship...Perhaps they've dreamed of me as I have dreamed of them...Perhaps, therein, may lie our joint salvation."

As you move through both takes of *Coyote Heart*—the poem and then the little story—be aware of your own thoughts and feelings regarding your fundamental connection with the natural world around you and specifically the animal kingdom. Sometimes it is within one's silent breathing and heart beat that there is a direct realization of one's relationship with such beings like a coyote.

At http://www.predatordefense.org/coyotes.htm, we read the following: "Dog-like in appearance and nature. Monogamous, devoted caregivers. Stunning, intelligent, playful, and affectionate. Coyotes are magnificent animals that are tragically persecuted and historically maligned. Coyotes were greatly revered by Navajo herders, who called them 'God's dog.'"

Hope you enjoy this reading and discover your own wisdom and connection with the universe.

Pete Majoy

Coyote Heart: Poem

I.

Like a pearl surfacing in an inkwell
the moon rises
            on the shoulders of the night,
and silhouetted
as if cut from her smooth incandescence
he too rises
            bathed in her entrancing stillness
whose light
            liquefies in his eyes
and
passing through his blood
to warm his heart
only to turn back
upward bound through his throat
which
            stretched forward
                  mouth pointing
                  in strained excess
returns to her
            as a howl.

Midwinter's cold respiration
slows down
and leafless trees
                  jagged veins
                  across

            her otherwise flawless face
are still
but upon the boulder dusted by snow
he reaches beyond his outstretched body
pulled by her gravity
his heart elevated
        and lodged in his throat
howls
    howls
        howls his longing.
They make love this way
until dawn when the light of reason
breaks the spell
and what seemed like only two
becomes a chorus of birds
and trees groaning in the wind like cellos.
The softness of her disappearance
             is so gentle
             as if considerate
that he simply contracts
and numbly jumps
      from his perch
leaving deep prints cookie-cutter clean
to disappear in the new falling snow.
One month follows another
and like tuning forks
they play a symmetry of feeling,
a symphony of blind adoration
as she searched him out
              within the forest
and found
    he howls his worship
    he howls his joy of being discovered

he howls the ecstasy
> of not having been forgotten
he howls the love
> which alone
> makes the long sun-blinding days
tolerable
> makes the moonless nights less inky
>> emptiness
for
> he prowls in her memory
> whose light shoots from his eyes
and

> she knows it
> waiting an eternity
> yet to begin.

II.

Some say
he'll be the last creature on earth...
and
some have referred to him

as God's dog...

and
some have misunderstood
        and underestimated him
like
they were never hungry
like
they were never in love
like
the moon had never been mistress to their desire
like
they never felt a cry, a wail...a howl
creep into their throats
from their guts deep, deep in their souls
afloat in the agony and the ecstasy,
the vulnerability,
the heart-pounding euphoria,
the cardial crunching grief
sinking and rising,
purified and terrified
under her search
in her torchlight.

Some say
he cast the stars into the firmament...
Some say

he indeed created it all,
the up and the down,
the left and the right,
the inside and the outside,
but
for sure
he howls for the displaced
'cause in his heart he knows
the curse of ignorance
the venom of violence
as
he fled extinction
tail burning
ribs splitting in the gunfire,
and
lying there in the dust
she covered him in her mournful aura.
He howls for the lonely
for through his veins
the sap of solitude drips slowly
and
he can hear his heartbeat in his feet
tender in the call of the wild.
He howls in glory
for she hears him,
she hears his heart carried aloft in his song and
that is all that is necessary
to redeem the awful mechanics of existence
and
the thoughtless repetition of the seasons.

15

Coyote Heart: Story
Part I

Coyote holds love and hope in his heart and senses the great sorrow, the immense emptiness on which they float like delicate bubbles.....Coyote closes her eyes to listen to the message massage her fur with both gentle whispers and sharper turbulent reminders. The wind is often her closest friend.

Coyote smells his own soul as it explores the desert looking for water like roots of a tree eye blindly searching for what it will always find for a time but both eventually stretch toward the sky. Coyote loves the darkness which gifts her with the moon for she understands the ebb and flow of all things, the pendulum of joy and grief that is always in a dance with itself. Coyote dreamed she had found one human who sat on a flat rock under a full moon during a light rainfall.

Coyote is more patient than the sun at night for he waits for his supper knowing it will offer itself simply and only because he waits forever. Coyote survives cause she's got smart bones whose hollow porous caverns howl and echo the beauty of life and the silent wisdom of the void.

Coyote looks at you with nightlight eyes unblinking as he sees what you know about yourself but cannot utter. Your eyes return the fire. Coyote sleeps in a dream hood while her slowly beating heart rests on her pups whose whimpers feed the night with promises it will never be alone.

Coyote tells the clouds that they are his thoughts and her feelings chasing each other across an endless sky disappearing behind their golden eyes. Coyote   plays with the stars lying on her back pawing the twinkling lights as if they were mobiles hanging over a child's crib and she smiles at them as if they were offspring.

Coyote travels the parched landscape in search of water and never stops even when he drinks from a stream for he knows that the rush of air against his whiskers is part of the quenching. Coyote leaves her paw prints on sand, mud, and the forest floor until the wind hides them under whatever it moves but the return does not depend on what she sees but what she knows, and she knows her prints are there forever.

Coyote digs for water on a cool surface wherein to lay his body. He licks the water that rises strained to purity by the earth, and he rests in the cool quarters he has dug from the same ground. His thoughts are his memories, but they seem to have always been there as if they were not to be remembered! Coyote howls at midnight with a restlessness of sexual need which she wants to fulfill but which must be delayed, and she fills the cosmos with a yearning that becomes a shooting star and she is fulfilled that the universe acknowledges!

Coyote knows that he creates the universe, the beauty, the love, the passion which so engages him. When he sees her, he knows she is a part of himself and that is why there is so much grieving in lost love for Coyote is left searching forever for a part of himself till he realizes it's still there, a bit tender but there. Coyote understands the grin of true joy and the grimace of true sorrow. She holds both masks upon her face and simply recognizes them when they are present. She grins at the grimaces and grimaces at the grin. They have become partners in her.

Coyote's heart is defenseless when it is touched by moonlight, caressed by comforting shade in a desert. The strength and directness of his response comes with the territory of being Coyote for he cannot but let life flow in all its wonders, joys, and sorrows. Coyote silently approaches the campfire of dreams, both hers and your own, and for awhile is content to gaze through the flames at the sleeper until there is a stirring and she feels she will soon disappear when the dreamer wakens so she walks off quietly not to break the dream forever.

Coyote rushes to the edge of the flowing rivulet and stops to play with his own reflection and to change the picture with his tongue as if it were a brush mixing and swirling paint on a canvas and through the ripples he sees her watching him from the depths. Coyote's longing can never completely find a care and so she makes of her longing the source of her great compassion as she follows the sun into the hidden cave of her heart and dwells there.

Coyote found the invisible path to the stars and his paws tingle along the way for the path is fire and the path is ice and the secret is to find the middle and that takes time and tingles. Coyote gives her heart unconditionally for she knows it is the only way one knows anything for what it is. She invites you to be yourself for there is no need to escape who you are as she looks at you.

Coyote drifts alone out of the woods onto the divided highway. In your car you see him waiting to cross and at the moment you pass him, his eyes give you love for without a blink they instantly surrender to your intentions leaving you naked in the truth. Coyote follows the trail of a moving snake through the shade of a pile of stones and stops. She intends no intrusion. She is not hungry. Her only intention is to follow and notice what is going on with the snake. She does this a lot with her own heart.

Coyote hears his own voice whisper to take the tough path, the one where you don't look behind and the one where you accept what was and don't try to change what is. He realizes there are some things which can only come cleanly, and should only come in total freedom or not at all. Coyote falls asleep under the stars with her eyes open. The stars only exist when she sees them, so she has learned to sleep this way comforted by their existence until she can bear it no longer, lets out a sigh and lets them go as she closes her eyes.

Coyote's heart almost ran through his chest when he saw her flash before his eyes as she suddenly appeared from behind the boulder. He said nothing as the sun united them in its warmth before they were distracted by the hawk. Coyote cried opalescent tears when she came upon his dead body minus the foot he chewed off to escape the trap set by the ones who smell funny. She licked his face and tasted the last of his soul before it rejoined the stars.

Coyote carried a heavy heart for days, weeks and months since he embraced the tough path. He had taught her what she was looking for, and in the process opened his heart. Coyote knew she would have to leave to find her own path down from the mesa. He could still hear her soft feet in the distance, vaguely. Coyote dreamed she had found one human who sat on a flat rock under a full moon during a light rainfall who understood Coyote. She dreamed of him running toward the moon cloud tears in his eyes smiling. She dreamed his smile all night and woke in the morning soaking wet.

Coyote dreamed he had become a man who sat on a rock facing the full moon during a light rainfall. He saw himself rising toward the moon filled with heavenly lacrimae smiling from a deep place in his heart. When he woke, he saw her staring at him as if he were a man who had become a coyote. Coyote sometimes slept lightly, aware of the creatures which walked and crawled near her. She was not a predator to them. Sometimes they would crawl or dance across her face and she'd bare a fang. They'd scamper, but she was not angry, only twitching from being tickled.

Coyote would walk for so many miles that length was no longer measured by distance but by time. He'd manage to forget her at a certain point and feel at peace with himself. But he's walked so far that he returned to the beginning place and she'd also returned having walked with him the whole time but silently, unobtrusively. Coyote retraces her steps back to where she left him howling at the moon. All she found were footprints, but they were left as impressions on her heart. She knew she would forever hear his call there.

Coyote has always faced the truth for to him there was only one way to walk, directly to one's prey, one's mate, one's howling space, one's sleep. His lungs fill with truth which he sings to the moon because she knows anyway. Coyote licks her paws to clean them of the dust gathered there from the long walk across the desert that appeared in her dreams the night before. At some point in time her dreams had become so real they left gifts.

Coyote has found a spot above the lowlands on a mesa that gives him energy.

He has this deep sense of where to stop to make friends with an area that seems alive and inviting. Because of this, he has many homes and many mothers. Coyote still twitched at night during certain dreams when he appeared to her as her teacher and passionate half of her half of her tender and passionate self. The moon was always full in these dreams and his back was always arched against it.

Coyote looked back at his tracks in the wet soil after he had walked forever in the heavy rains that fell from empty skies that had not filled with clouds for days and days. He realized that the rain had preceded and followed him as a reminder. Its sound was endless memory and he was soaking wet under its power. Coyote has no final resting place. Coyote has no final rest. Coyote has seen the sunshine through her paws on the hot ground and smelled the ocean through her tail wagged by offshore breezes. She is everywhere and nowhere.

Coyote knows the deep darkness, the connecting emptiness, and the rich soil under all that appears. He knows it connects us all and is that out of which we spring to our feet to hunt the moon, to chase our tails, to listen to the whale songs from this ocean of bliss and this cosmos of attention. Coyote has learned the lesson of letting go which she rehearses every day. She controls nothing yet has power over everything because she has recognized who she is. She caught a glimpse of herself when she followed her howl as it disappeared into everywhere which she could never find.

Coyote feels the heat fill her body as he turns into the wilderness knowing no set return. He senses he will be led back by the same person that calls him forth. It is the sound of her voice that calls from the rocks where iguanas bathe. Coyote fills her day with thoughts of everything imaginable and nothing at all. Her mind floats upon the wind empty and full, free and limited, fulfilled and yearning, a leaf newly formed and one suddenly fallen. She changes position in the shadow of the tree.

Coyote walked without identity until he disappeared from self-knowledge. At that moment leaving paw prints between the caves whose shadows offered relief from the sun, he knew he had escaped from the desert of self-concern and pulled into an oasis of love. Coyote waited for him in the desire of her heart and the passion which kept watch in her body. She felt him loving her in the distance and she suddenly turned as she felt his face brush hers but it was only the wind with his heart written on it. Come to me, come to me she howled, I am your servant, I am your master.

Coyote searched the sand for inscriptions, for residue of hieroglyphics etched in the night winds. He stopped at a perfect circle that was disappearing from the crawling sand as fast as it was formed. He stood in the center and fell asleep waking up only when the sand was about to cover his mouth. For days granules remained in his fur, a constant reminder of the circle of endless days of yearning. Coyote's heart burns like the residue as from a pile of thrown away leaves and timber whose fire has been reduced to a glow that fades and alternately brightens from sudden winds that embraces it. It is the way of a coyote heart never to burn out, never to be free of the melancholy the heart lives in when touched by love and the yearning it leaves behind.

Coyote paws the dirt around a burnt out fire left by a pair of drifters, two hearts that traveled inside their mutual longing and outside their separate bodies, and he searches for a message in the soot, like a seer studying tea leaves or coffee grinds hoping for a trace of their satisfaction, but he lopes away in his own emptiness into the pink twilight. Coyote stared into the sinking sun which tucked itself in behind a misty sheet of fog at the edge of the world. He felt a singularity of purpose. He was simply there as a witness. There was the sun. There he was. That was all. He was witness to two great events: the setting sun and the setting heart. Both would rise again the next day. He was, therefore, witness to hope.

PART II

Coyote has observed his breath, how it changes with a perception of movement behind the high mesa even if it be only dust, even if the movement be utter stillness which seems to be kinetic though it is simply there as the stage on which thought dances, Coyote's thought alive in his breath, his rhythm, life in, life out, in, out, every moment, his closest friend. Coyote leaves his prints behind and hears them whispering to him that they are memories of where he was and that they neither praise nor blame him for what he was but urges him to consider only the present, the prints in the making.

Coyote wanders into a thicket of blueberry bushes and rests near their roots shaded from the sun. He nibbles a berry for its tartness and falls asleep. He dreams of how it happened that he became such a wanderer and wakes up to a shooting star visible partly through the bush. Coyote senses the passage of time as the unpicked berries wither on the bush. He senses the movement of time as he rises to seek a moon and a high place to howl. He is called by some force to represent the longing of the heart, the endless repetition of Coyote chanting into the infinite universe, the way his dignity approaches the restless quality of life, a life in passing, passing away, as it should.

Coyote suddenly finds his hind quarters yelping in pain as the black bear sliced through his loins sending him hurtling down a rocky embankment coming to a stop beside a river. His head was bleeding through his left ear but he was breathing very slowly, almost dead as the water whispered cleansing to his wounds and his soul left his body for a time. Coyote entered his own heart pulsing noiselessly at the rim of nowhere, a nowhere which was everything a heart could stand that knew the universe was not a void of meaninglessness but a mass of eternal centers of awareness. She could feel her heart—it was light as a feather , full without body, without limit.

Coyote senses the absence of his senses and in their absence senses even more acutely all that he had sensed before the bear came. He is fully present to all coyotes, even watchful of their wandering days and nights through the light snow pock-marked with deer tracks and he knows that never has a deer disappeared at the will of coyotes except by necessity, obedience to cosmic law. Coyotes' steps are as long as galaxies, as quick as waking from sleep. Her eyes have watched the sun, a million suns, without burning up and she came to realize she had been given a great gift. No sun, no star is more intense than a single heart filled with love, overflowing with compassion reaching out toward the beloved in the exuberance and immediacy of the moment of innocence and pleasure.

Coyote knows he is a phantom, that his warm paws and seasoned fur wrapped around the sleek sinews of tissue, muscle and bone lay still beside the rumbling river, just the appearance of sleep, just the silence of his soulless corpse still warm waiting for his return as if it still were really his to possess. Coyote feels the anonymity of love because it knows no boundaries, selects no worthy recipient, withdraws from nobody, as if love itself had simply filled his heart with infinite proportions which are no proportions at all. He struggles against his own selfishness only to discover that he himself is embraced in the warmth which has filled him and massaged his limitations.

Coyote migrates through the ether pulling back the curtain separating him from his body and he can hear the river lapping at his paws, teasing his fur, talking to his underbelly, and soon the river is gone and he becomes the river spying on a near dead coyote floating downstream like a rag. Coyote has been stopped in her tracks to face the ultimate acceptance, the impermanence of all things, and she feels the sensation of drifting half asleep upon a gentle, loving, purposeful stream heading back to life, getting ready for a new shore upon which to rise to a fresh awareness that there is really nothing to fear, nothing!

Coyote relaxes in the twilight body of lightness knowing in his weightless sinews that there is never satisfaction in either companionship or solitude unless the terrible emptiness is allowed to challenge one's anxious attempts to simply fill it up. Coyote knows that companionship and aloneness are both gifts of letting go of expectations. Coyote watches her body floating upon the river current hardly disturbing the surface tension of the water and she is filled with compassion, that loving wisdom, that insight into the condition of conditioning, the struggle she has had to just be a coyote, to just be herself, absent of all expectations, all goals, everything.

Coyote, remembered by his empty flesh, sees across time and space and knows how narrow is our vision, the contracted time and space he lived in before the bear struck. Coyote sees his courage and the heart of all who live before the bear strikes, and he sees why we have reason to be proud. Coyote sits in her infinite bliss, the stillness at the core of action, the soul of each sparkle of energy and life, and comes to know the wisdom of everlasting joy, that all that is---is splendor, even the pain, even the decomposition that may be setting is within her almost rigid body whose warmth has almost totally exited above the eyebrows above the eyes that have seen more than just data.

Coyote wakes beside the stream, black bear holding his head softly ministering to his pain with his complete concern that the encounter was only in the nature of things, nothing personal. When Coyote understood, black bear swam to the other shore forever. Coyote returns to her breath half alive, half dead at the border between past and future when she hears a howl across the river and knows again the chanting of the great awareness and the love that holds them gently.

Coyote licked his wounds between howls and the movement of the silent river shot reflections of the moon toward both shores, toward each of them as owls hooed and wolves heard their heartbeats and the forest exploded in a harmony of open throats. Coyote saw, smelled and heard the silence afresh not just as the pause between howls but as the howls themselves. Her howls were so soundless and soothingly quiet at their very heart. That night she sang her silence and the stars blinked their agreement.

Coyote heals slowly here, quickly there, stretching his limbs elastic in their sinewy reach but his heart lands upon the other shore first before his paw and that's how it will be for awhile. After all, he thought, isn't that the way it always is in the land of heart's imagining. Coyote is in no rush to fully resurrect from her death. A piece of her soul still drifts apart from her body, still free to run the river, still free to haunt the other shore, still free in the nether space of his dreams where she howls her love song.

Coyote wakens before dawn. He lifts himself to gaze through the thickest of trees just barely in contrast to the gradually disappearing darkness and knows the path between them which he takes to the river's edge. He stops. There is a sound behind him. He pays no attention and drinks. His footsteps arrived late to his ears. Coyote felt the first shade of light through her body before her eyes caught the sun sliced through the trees into a multitude of mist reflecting rays. She took a deep breath and with it, inhaled the last of her soul. Thirsty as he had been, she too slowly trotted to the water and stopped. She drank the vision of his body on the other river bank.

Coyote felt his image, a refreshing libation, swallowed in deep awareness and great enchantment, a temporary arrangement of his likeness, a fluid icon of nourishment that lifted her spirits which he could see as the current ever so slowly edged her river reflection under his eyes as they gazed downward before his lips kissed her face. Coyote knew again as she had always known that the river always widened and the exchange of the dream spell mediated by the river would be more difficult and chances were greater that their reflections would disappear in the longer journey between shores. But, their howls would always tell their story and share their appreciation and the underlying understanding that there never really was any distance between their hearts....

Inter-Being/Inter-Dependence and Ecological Reflections

In the October 20, 2012 edition of *Psychology Today*, an article appeared titled "Coyotes: Let's Appreciate America's Song Dog," written by Marc Bekoff, Ph.D. in which he begins this way: "Coyote, America's song dog, is an amazing and magnificent animal who is very misunderstood, historically maligned, and tragically and reprehensibly persecuted. Coyotes are intelligent, playful, affectionate, and devoted caregivers. Native Americans appreciated them as cunning tricksters. They are among the most adaptable animals on Earth and are critical to the integrity of many diverse ecosystems."

The notion of "inter-being" and "inter-dependence" is quite simple and true. Nothing exists completely independent of/from everything else whether it be we human beings, animals, fish, earth, air and water. We are all connected and dependent on each other. Thich Nhat Hanh tells us this: "Impermanence is the context of transformation of things. Without impermanence, there can be no life. Selflessness is the interdependent nature of all things. Without interdependence, nothing could exist." This raises the question regarding our connection with animals like a coyote and why so much violence against animals like the coyote has taken place. You can do research that proves that the killing of animals like coyotes because they supposedly were a menace in attacking livestock owned by farmers is a myth that has been embraced by the USDA (United States Department of Agriculture). This same myth has been used regarding coyote attacks on people. Mark Bekoff states that coyotes "have a healthy respect for people and actually avoid us almost all the time."

So, what can we learn from this? If we are interdependent which includes the relationship between human beings and animals, what conclusions can we arrive at that promote respect, care, and nurturing of animal life around us? When you slowly but surely ingest information about the wonder-world of coyotes, what arises within oneself regarding the inter-being/inter-dependence between us and animals in general. How does the treatment of animals influence human existence/survival here on planet earth.

Lastly, the connection between coyotes and our eco-system. Mr. Bekoff states this: "...coyotes play a critical role in keeping natural areas healthy. In fact, coyotes are considered to be a keystone species, meaning that their presence or absence has a significant impact on the surrounding biological community. For instance, because coyotes reduce the number of nest predators and jackrabbits, sage grouse benefits include higher chick survival and less competition for food....By exerting a top down regulation of other species, coyotes maintain the balance in the food web below and around them. When coyotes are absent or even just greatly reduced in a natural area, the relationships between species below them in the web are altered, putting many small species at risk...It's clear and inarguable that we should respect coyotes for whom they are and appreciate that they still bless our lives....Peaceful existence is easy to accomplish and we should all aspire to having more harmonious relationships with the amazing beings with whom we share our homes as we head into the future."

In the long run, as Native Americans have shown us, our life here on Earth is deeply connected to the animals that live here with us. There is much that we can learn from them and from each other about cooperating in the survival of our world by living in peace including a peace that is shared with the animal kingdom.

Biography

Peter Majoy's devotion to human rights, to learning, and to educating others began as Clinic Supervisor of New York's first Methadone Maintenance Program at Richmond Memorial Hospital, Staten Island, in 1976, and continued as a public school teacher in several public school systems in the New York, New Jersey, and New England areas, culminating in the founding of SNTAS/NESA at Nashua High, NH. This school-within-a-school program pursued the *Paideia Proposal** by Mortimer Adler, and became involved with the *Coalition of Essential Schools*, which reflected the groundbreaking, anti-bureaucratic school concepts of Thayer Academy's Dennis Litky.

Nominated by Holmdel High School in Holmdel, N.J. for *Princeton's Award for Distinguished Secondary School Teaching*, and with educational achievement and degrees in philosophy, theology, and English education, Majoy's life has been, and remains, devoted to the education of the mind, the soul, and the heart.

**National Paideia Center Declaration of Principles:*

All children are educable;

<>Education is never completed in school or higher institutions of learning, but is a lifelong process of maturity for all citizens;

<>The primary cause of learning is the activity of the child's mind, which is not created by, but only assisted by the teacher;

<>Multiple types of learning and teaching must be utilized in education, not just teacher lecturing, or telling;

<>A student's preparation for earning a living is not the primary objective of schooling.

PUBLICATIONS

(All available at Amazon.com)

Doorways to Learning: A Model for Developing the Brain's Full Potential (1993 by Zephyr Press)

Riding the Crocodile, Flying the Peach Pit: A Sensory Approach to Education (1996 by Zephyr Press)

Coyote Heart (2018 by Brainjoy-Create Space, Amazon).
Based on Much of What We Know About Coyotes and What Others Have Wonderfully Written About Them, This Small Booklet is a Brief Journey Into a Coyote's Heart, a Wonderful Metaphor Regarding Our Own Human Hearts. 40 pages.

REVIVED & FORTHCOMING in 2018

Hair Pin Turns Fourteen Stories for Imaginative and Thankful Learning. Written for use by teachers. 123 pages.

The Accepting One Four Essays and Equally Lengthy Meditations and Reflections About Each Chapter with a Focus on Life on Earth, Where It is Going, and What Our Role Is. 33 pages.

The Compassionate One: Gifts From the Blue-Green Dimension
Written in 1986 With Some Editing Through the Years. It was completed After 15 Consecutive Mornings of Meditation and Writing.. As Stated in the Book: "It is our compassion which makes all the difference both individually and as a small planet in one solar system in an almost infinite universe." 106 Pages

The Dust From Which We all Shall Rise Eleven Connected Poems About Life, Death, and Transcendence. 41 pages.

The Rhythms of This and That Collection of Many Poems from 1981 to 2018, Focused on Direct Experiences That are Personal, Political, and Global in Nature. 79 pages.

Simon Says Twelves Short Stories About Growing Up, the Various and Interconnected Experiences That Help Us Understand Each Other and Ourselves, and a Character, Benjy Moss, Who Appears in a Number of Roles Throughout the Book. 94 pages.

Free Range Play in Dream-Time A Comical Book for Youngsters That Can be Used at an Elementary School (Grades 4-8). It is Essentially About a Multitude of Experiences on Many Levels, Often Very Silly but Sometimes Not So. Much of the Book Uses Visual Experiences to More Deeply Understand their Thoughts and Feelings About Each Chapter. 49 Pages.

Sunny Boy A Novel About Male and Female Identity and the Perceptions, Both Positive and Negative, that Genders have About Each Other. It is Sometimes Funny, Often Vulgar, Quasi Porno, and at Moments Very Insightful. 117 Pages.

(All are copyrighted and available in 2018 in pre-published format as Brainjoy Publications.)

Contact:

Peter W. Majoy
143 S. Lincoln St.
Keene, NH 03431
(603) 352-4438
ptmjoy@gmail.com

FUTURE PUBLICATIONS

A Teacher's Guide to Whole Brain Learning *Finished in 1987 but
needs* Editing and Only a Few Updates. Intended for Teachers at All
Levels and Subjects. It is a Very Direct Helping Guide to Teaching,
Especially if Teaching Makes One Happy and Thankfully Aware That
He/She Loves to Teach.

Brian In Da Hood: Da Hood Be Wisdom, Inc. A Humorous Book
About my   Communication With My Son, Brian, When He Was 21
And I Was 54. It is Hilarious, Heart Moving, and Wonderful.

Cruel Truths: A Journey Through Divorce The Particular and
Global Experience of Divorce

***The Context of Our Lives: The Mental Model of the World Around
Us and Its Effect and Affect on How We Live*** Up to Part III With a
Total of 5-6 Sections to Complete the First Draft. Includes a Large
Chapter on Interstellar Relationships, i.e., the Heart and Soul of UFO
Encounters..

The Paradigm Shift of Sustainable Energy Evolution A Socio-
Political-Ecological View of Models of Thinking Which Need to Evolve
if Our Earth Home Will Survive. It is a Kind of Follow-Up to The
Context of Our Lives.

Peter Majoy